Coming to School
IS REALLY
COOL!

By
**Sandy Ragona &
Stefani Weber, M.Ed.**

© 2014, 2007 by YouthLight, Inc.
Chapin, SC 29036

Cover Design and Layout by Diane Florence
Graphic Assistance by Amy Rule
Project Editing by Susan Bowman

ISBN: 9781598500219

Library of Congress Number
2007920026

10 9 8 7 6 5 4 3 2
Printed in the United States

Acknowledgements

I would like to thank Youthlight, Inc. for their support with this book. From the inception of the idea, Youthlight, Inc. has provided guidance and encouragement to make this book a reality. I thank my husband Andy for his patience and his encouragement to actualize my dreams of writing books. He is my sounding board and best friend. To Stef, my counseling collegue, a big thank you for the sharing of lessons and cooperative efforts in publish our best practices for increasing school attendance.

- Sandy Ragona

I would like to thank Bob and Sue Bowman for giving me this opportunity to write my first book. To Sandy Ragona, for keeping me on a writing schedule, setting deadlines for us, and for her encouragement. Without her, I would have procrastinated much more! To my colleagues at Kennedy and Irving Schools, who are so supportive of our guidance program and our professional efforts. Most importantly, I would like to thank my uncle, John Petrakis, who encouraged me to get a good education and to use my education to serve others. Thank you all for helping me to achieve one of my life's goals – to be a published author!

- Stef Weber

Dedication

This book is dedicated to our children who need our help to value education and to see attending school as a priority.

This book is also dedicated to adults who work diligently to expound ways and means to increase student attendance. We know that school attendance is the beginning to achieving a good education and to actualizing dreams for the future.

It is our hope that you will use the activities in this book to help every child view school attendance as the most important job in their life.

- Sandy Ragona

This book is dedicated to all those students and families who have allowed me to be part of their life and learning over the past thirty years. To my son, J.C., who has challenged me to think outside the box, which has helped me in my work with children.

- Stef Weber

Table of Contents

Introduction

Absenteeism is a problem in every school to some degree. This book was written to be proactive with attendance issues. Helping students with absenteeism before it becomes a problem is important. By starting in elementary school, *Coming To School IS Really COOL!* can help students to understand cause and effect and to take personal responsibility for their attendance.

When there is chronic absenteeism it affects everyone – school culture, parents, classroom climate and the community. According to Holbert, Wu and Stark, 2002, "Interventions that start in elementary school, according to some studies, are more effective in increasing attendance then starting in middle or ninth grade." Ford and Stephen (1996) suggest, "Working to help a child establish a positive relationship with the school system in the earliest grades would seem to be more feasible than working to rectify a negative relationship when the child becomes an adolescent."

Truancy has been identified as one of the early warning signs of students with the potential for delinquent activity, social isolation or educational failure from dropping out, suspension or expulsion (Huizinga, D., Loeber, R. Thornberry, T.P., 2000). Lack of commitment to school has been shown by several studies as a risk factor for delinquency, school dropout, substance abuse and teen pregnancy (US Department of Health, 2001; Blum, R., Beuhring and Rinehart, 2000; Huizinga, Loeber, Thornberry, and Cothern, 2000). "Chronic truancy in elementary school is linked to serious delinquent behavior at age 12 and under" (Loeber and Farrington, 2000).

High rates of truancy have been linked to daytime burglary and vandalism. (Baker, 2000) "60 percent of juvenile crime occurred between 8 a.m. and 3 p.m. weekdays" (Truancy Justice Bulletin, 2001). The financial impact of truancy and dropouts can be measured by the business loss because of youth who "hang out" and/or shoplift during the day, higher rates of crime, and the cost of social services for families of children who are habitually truant. "Truancy, however, has an even more direct financial impact on communities: the loss of Federal and State education funding" (Juvenile Justice Bulletin, 2001). As of 1997, 41 % of prison inmates and 31% of probationers eighteen years and older had not graduated from high school or earned a GED, compared with 18% of the general population. (Harlow, C.W., 2003). The average dropout costs $200,000.00 over the cost of his/her lifetime. (Vernez, Krop, Rydell, 1999).

Knowing the cause and effect of absenteeism and understanding the federal mandate, No Child Left Behind, schools need to take action. *Coming To School IS Really COOL!* is a manual to increase school attendance based on current research, which meets the NCLB requirements. Within this book, you will find a variety of activities/lesson designs that can be used for individuals, or small or large groups.

Coming To School IS Really COOL! will build a strong foundation for elementary students to understand that attendance is very important to success in school. They will develop skills to increase their confidence, internal locus of control, and ability to maximize their school attendance. Educators need to help students see the correlation between the cause and effect of attendance and academic success and growth.

Introduction (cont.)

Coming To School IS Really COOL! has three components: student, school and parent. The student component is made up of the strategies and goals within ten lessons that students can use to help themselves attend school regularly. In the Addendum, the school and parent components are discussed in greater detail. The school component discusses strategies educators can use to create a warm, caring and challenging classroom and school environment. Helping parents to understand the importance of school attendance and working with school personnel to create a cooperative relationship is the essence of the parent component.

When researching best practices to remediate attendance problems, there was limited current research-based information to be found. In writing this book, information dated after 2000 was used, as well as books, interviews with judges and truancy officers. The research that was gathered and used is presented in the Need For This Book section.

Need for This Book

Educators know that chronic absenteeism contributes to a student's lack of academic growth and friends. The cause and effect of not attending school leads to failure in the academic and social worlds. Decades of research indicate that children who have chronically unexcused absences are at risk for having more serious behavioral issues such as substance abuse, involvement in criminal activity, and incarceration (Baker, Sigmon, & Nugent, 2001). These at-risk behaviors are the reasons that schools need effective interventions to increase student attendance.

Three questions to reflect on when looking at why absenteeism is a concern are:

 How can we help students change the problems with coming to school?

 How can we create a school where high expectations engage all students in a culture of support and respect?

 How can we get parental support so that parents will bring their children to school on a regular basis?

The pressure to intervene on the issue of absenteeism is now a federal mandate. The federal government made attendance an "additional indicator" for elementary and middle schools to meet Adequate Yearly Progress (AYP) for the No Child Left Behind Act (NCLB, 2002). For the full text of this provision, see NCLB, Title I, Part A, Section IIII (b), 2C at www.ed.gov/policy/elsec/leg/esea02/pg2.html#sec1111. Districts are now required to report unexcused absences to the state. Statistics show that absenteeism due to reasons other than illness and cutting individual classes increases with each grade level, starting in the eighth grade. (National Center for Education Services, 2002)

A broader view of attendance issues, which is becoming more prevalent in educational literature, is that attendance is an indicator of larger, more complex issues of disengagement and student motivation, and that school culture and structure contribute to both (Bryk & Thurn, 1989; Lan & Lanthier, 2003; Lee & Burkam, 2003). Studies still stress the importance of parents and students remaining accountable for attendance. There is a need for schools to take a serious look at the climate, culture, and academics and how these affect attendance problems.

Parental support is a key issue in attendance problems. Thirty years of research has consistently linked family involvement to higher student achievement, better attitudes toward school lower dropout rates, increased attendance, and many other positive outcomes for students, families, and schools (Henderson & Mapp, 2002).

How To Use This Book

This book can be easily adapted for several settings: individual or small or large groups. Elementary teachers, counselors, and other educators can pick up this book and use its ten strategies with minimal preparation.

Each of the ten lessons teaches a skill which will help the student to become more responsible for their school attendance. As a unit, the entire series of lessons can be presented in five weeks or spread out in ten weeks throughout the year. Each lesson will help you to teach students the value of coming to school regularly.

Five Easy Steps to Using this Book:

1 Display the poster.

2 Introduce the lesson.

3 Discuss questions/activities.

4 Complete the student activity sheet.

5 Send home student initiated parent info-gram.

Lessons

Lesson One: The Things I Like about School
Lesson Two: The Importance of Coming to School
Lesson Three: Tough Times
Lesson Four: Goals to Improve Attendance
Lesson Five: *Coming to School IS Really COOL!* (Rap Song)
Lesson Six: Student Responsibilities at Home

How To Use This Book (cont.)

Lesson Seven: Time Management
Lesson Eight: Success/Money
Lesson Nine: How Attendance Impacts the Future
Lesson Ten: Interview
Addendum: Student and Parent Checklists

What is in Each Lesson?

Coming To School IS Really COOL! is a book with complete lesson design and activities. Each skill in each lesson comes complete with a student activity sheet; follow-up questions, personal testimonials, student info-gram to parent(s).

⭐ **Student Activities:**
These reproducible activities can be used to teach and/or reinforce the lessons.

⭐ **Follow-up Questions/Discussions:**
Questions help to transfer skills into real life experiences. Teacher/counselor may use these questions to check for understanding and clarity of each lesson.

⭐ **Personal Testimonials:**
These statements or stories shared by the teacher/counselor help students to understand the ways others problem-solve similar situations.

⭐ **Student Info-gram:**
These reproducible info-grams are an easy way to share with parents the lessons their child has learned in school. These info-grams are student-initiated notes to their parents.

Addendum

I. School Responsibility

Perhaps the most important finding in research concerning dropout prevention, attendance, student engagement, and effective small schools is that students are more likely to remain and achieve in schools where people care about them (Bernard, 2004; Green, 1998;Steinberg & Allen, 2002;Wimberly, 2002).

A. Caring environment

•Greet students and their families when they arrive at school/classroom. Make them feel welcome.

Call immediately: When students are absent, please talk with a family member to inquire about their child. Let them know that you are concerned and hope to see them back in school soon.

Upon return: When students return to school, let them know how much you missed them. Talk with them about why they missed school and offer help for problems or assistance to catch up academically.

•Recognize good attendance by putting it on the announcements or website, posting around school, or sites where everyone goes such as the gym, library or lunch room. Recognize GOOD attendance not just perfect attendance.

•Some students may not be coming to school because they are afraid. They may be afraid of being bullied by other students, making mis takes or other such things.

•Create an environment of respect for everyone. Let students know if they speak up, an adult will listen and take appropriate action.

•Refer students with family problems to the school counselor or administrator. They will refer the family to services that will help.

•Have high expectations for students. Focus on student strengths and challenge them to work on their areas of weakness.

•Using rewards in the classroom has mixed results according to research. Provide students with an internal locus of control for their achievements.

•Provide collaborative learning opportunities for students. These activities are motivating. They engage students directly in the learning process and help them get to know one another thereby, decreasing bullying.

Addendum *(cont.)*

II. Parent Connection (Power of the family)

When perceived problems with absences is linked to limited or inconsistent parent involvement, interventions that can be used include:

A. Home visits

1. School Prep Routines – help parents to establish routines.
    a. Morning Routines
        Wake up time
        Breakfast
        Bath/Shower if not done in evening
        Dress
        Brush Teeth, comb hair
        Get backpack, coat
        Leave home time/catch bus time
        Transportation backup plan
    b. Evening Routines
        Snack
        Homework time
        Play
        Dinner
        Bath/Shower
        Brush teeth
        Reading together (10-20 minutes)
        Bedtime (no television)
    c. Child's room
        No television
        Minimal toys
        Books are fine

2. Counsel parents to see the importance of school attendance and household routines.
    a. Telephoning parents to problem solve and develop better strategies to attend school regularly.

III. Student Responsibility

A. The ten lessons help students learn their responsibilities.

Lesson 1

TOP TEN THINGS I LIKE ABOUT SCHOOL

Lesson 1

TOP TEN THINGS I LIKE ABOUT SCHOOL

Lesson One

Top Ten Things
I Like About School

Description:
➝This lesson is designed to identify interests and activities that students enjoy about school.

Objective(s):
➝Students will learn about their interests/activities that motivate their school attendance.

Estimated Time:
➝30 minutes

Material(s) Needed:
➝School Questionnaire (Screening Tool) (see page 24)
➝Top Ten Activity Sheet (see page 26)
➝Parent Thank You Note (see page 19)
➝Draw a Cool School sheet (see page 20)
➝Things I would like to Change Sheet (see page 21)
➝Poster template (see page 22)
➝Info gram to the principal (see page 23)

Procedures:
➝Have students complete the Screening Tool (independently or read aloud) to identify how students feel about school/home and how they see themselves. (Using this screening tool will provide pertinent information that could send up a red flag for additional consultation with other educators.)

16

Lesson One

Top Ten Things
I Like About School *(cont.)*

➛Discuss how our interests/likes motivate us to work hard. Talk about the feelings that enjoyment brings at school.
➛Have students complete the activity sheet.

➛Summarize the findings by:
  •Why are the likes/interests on the list?
  •How do these likes/interests motivate you to come to school?

➛Have students color the introduction sheet on page 15 and fill in the thank you to their parent(s).

Follow-up Discussion:
➛Identify feelings associated with the interests/activities.
➛Talk with students about their parent(s) job of getting them to school on time.
➛Use poster template as a coloring page, a story starter, a what if situation or any other way that would enhance the message of the lesson.

Personal Testimonial:
➛Share how your interests/likes motivate you to work hard.

Lesson One

 **Top Ten Things I Like About School**

1. _____

2. _____

3. _____

4. _____

5. _____

6. _____

7. _____

8. _____

9. _____

10. _____

Lesson One

Top Ten Things
I Like About School

Dear _____,

Thank you for getting me to school on time.

While I am at school, I like _____,

_____, and _____.

Love,

_____

The Ideal
COOL School

Create a picture showing your ideal "Cool School". Be sure to include all the things you feel would make a school the BEST. Have fun!

Things I Would Change Worksheet

Here is your opportunity! Make a list or draw the things you feel need to be changed at school to make our school "Really Cool". Tell how these changes would help our school to be a better place for everyone.

Change	Reason for Change

Poster
Template

INFO-GRAM
CHANGE IS NEEDED

Dear _____, (principal)
We have been studying about school – the things we like and the things we think will make our school a better place for everyone. Here are some of the things I think need to be changed at _____ School:

_____

_____

_____.

I hope you will think about these ideas to make our school a better place. I would be happy to meet with you to talk about how we could make these changes happen. Thanks for considering our ideas.

                Sincerely,

                _____

School Questionnaire

Top Ten Things I Like About School

Please check yes or no to answer the following questions.

❏ **Yes** ❏ **No**　1.　Do you think that school is fun?

❏ **Yes** ❏ **No**　2.　Do you feel scared to talk in front of your classmates?

❏ **Yes** ❏ **No**　3.　When schoolwork is hard, do you try harder?

❏ **Yes** ❏ **No**　4.　Do you feel scared at home?

❏ **Yes** ❏ **No**　5.　Do you have friends at school?

❏ **Yes** ❏ **No**　6.　Do others make fun of you?

❏ **Yes** ❏ **No**　7.　Do you get upset when you don't understand the assignment?

❏ **Yes** ❏ **No**　8.　Do you play games at recess?

❏ **Yes** ❏ **No**　9.　Is your school a happy place?

❏ **Yes** ❏ **No**　10. Are there problems in your neighborhood?

❏ **Yes** ❏ **No**　11. Do you eat breakfast?

❏ **Yes** ❏ **No**　12. Do you think you are as smart as the other kids in your class?

❏ **Yes** ❏ **No**　13. Do you have a homework/work space at home?

❏ **Yes** ❏ **No**　14. Do you feel comfortable in your classroom?

❏ **Yes** ❏ **No**　15. Do you have friends to play with at home?

Lesson 2: School is Important!!

TOP TEN REASONS TO COME TO SCHOOL

Lesson 2: School is Important!!

Lesson Two

Top Ten Reasons to Come to School

Description:
→This lesson will teach students the importance of coming to school.

Objective(s):
→Students will learn reasons to attend school regularly.
→Students will understand the cause and effect of good attendance.

Estimated Time:
→45 minutes

Material(s) Needed:
→Brainstorming School Is Important Web (see page 29)
→Journal/Color Activity Sheet (see page 32)
→Parent News Gram (see page 30)
→Use poster template as a coloring page, a story starter, a what if situation or any other way that would enhance the message of the lesson.

Procedures:
→Disseminate the handout: "School Is Important Web" (page 29)

→Brainstorm questions and complete web.
      Why I should come to school?
      How coming to school will help me?
      What happens when I don't miss school?

Lesson Two

Top Ten Reasons to Come to School *(cont.)*

➤Handout Journal/Color Activity Sheet.

Procedures:
➤Instruct students to write about their view of school's importance.

➤Have students color and complete Parent News Gram.

Follow-up Discussion:
➤Collate journal/color activity sheets for a classroom book, *Coming To School IS Really COOL!*
➤Contact someone from your school or community to share their own testimonial regarding the importance of school.
➤Why Is School Important? Activity sheet- web with one big circle, surrounded by 5 circles.

Personal Testimonial:
➤Share how good attendance helps you as an educator.

School is
Important

Lesson Two

BREAKING NEWS:
School Is Important

Dear _____,

Did you know: Good school attendance will

_____. When I

don't miss school, I _____

_____.

School is important because_____

_____.

Thanks, _____, for getting

me to school everyday.

Love,

_____

Journal Importance of School

Top Ten Reasons to Come to School

Why should I come to school?

_____

_____

_____

How can I get better at coming to school?

_____

_____

_____

How will getting to school on time help me?

_____

_____

_____

What happens when I don't miss school?

_____

_____

_____

Journal/Coloring Activity Sheet

 **Top Ten Reasons to Come to School**

School is important because:

_____

_____

Lesson 3

TOUGH TIMES

Lesson 3

TOUGH TIMES

Lesson Three

Tough Times

Description:
-In this lesson, students will understand how to motivate themselves when aspects of school are hard.

Objective(s):
-Students will identify _____ difficult aspects of school.
-Students will learn strategies to increase their efforts.

Estimated Time:
-30 minutes

Material(s) Needed:
-Tough Times Activity Sheet (see page 42)
-Parent Help Me Note (see page 41)
-Use poster template as a coloring page, a story starter, a what if situation or any other way that would enhance the message of the lesson.

Procedures:
-Read the Tough Times Story and discuss Follow-up Questions.
-Have students complete the activity sheet.
-Make a tough times goal with something that your students can work on as a class. Post the goal in your room and discuss progress daily.

Lesson Three

Tough Times

Personal Testimonial:
➨Share a time in your life when you never gave up even though you wanted to.

Follow up questions:
➨What did you learn from this story?
➨What did Carlos help Jon with to build confidence?
➨How can you apply these skills to your life?

Lesson 3

TOUGH TIMES STORY

Everyday when Jon walked to school, he was thinking about reading and math. He knew that when Mrs. Chan asked him to read in front of his classmates, he would be scared. You see reading was difficult for Jon.

As Jon opened the front door and entered the building he thought, "I finished my math homework, but I'm not sure if it is right." Jon doubted his ability and believed that he couldn't do as well as other students in his class.

Jon sat next to Carlos in the second row of his class. Sometimes they talked to each other during free time.

Lesson 3

TOUGH TIMES STORY

Each time Mrs. Chan assigned new story questions. Jon noticed that Carlos worked on the assignments quickly without any hesitation. Jon would watch him and wondered why he was so confident about school.

At recess, Jon would play soccer with his classmates. Everyone would run, block and kick, especially Carlos. He would steal the ball from the other team and quickly kick for a score.

Jon walked off the field with Carlos after the game was over.

"Hey, Jon," Carlos said. "Next time I will pass you the ball near the goalie, okay?"

Hesitating, Jon replied, "Do you think I will be able to score?"

Carlos stopped with a puzzled look on his face. "Of

TOUGH TIMES STORY

course you'll be able to score. If you believe you can, you will! If you think it's tough it will be hard. All you have to do is put in more effort, you know push yourself harder, and great things will happen."

Carlos walked away leaving Jon to rethink that confidence is created by pushing yourself when something is hard. Never giving up. With a little more effort, he thought, I will be successful in the classroom and on the soccer field.

Each day, Jon worked at his confidence. He pushed himself to read more, practicing the skills he learned in class. He ran faster on the soccer field too. Each time the soccer ball was close to him, he made a move to steal it from the other team. Twice he was successful.

Lesson 3

TOUGH TIMES STORY

After a few weeks, Jon received his reading grade, which was better than the last grading period. He knew his effort and hard work were paying off. He even asked Mrs. Chan if he could be the first to read aloud for the class.

As Carlos and Jon walked out to recess together, Carlos asked, "Are you ready for the game today?"

Quickly Jon replied, "You bet! If you send the ball my way, I will score. I know I can."

Carlos and Jon ran down the field, side by side. Carlos received the ball from a teammate, kicked it to Jon near the goal just as Jon thought, here is my chance. Jon kicked the ball high in the air and over the head of the goalie, straight into the net. Cheers from everyone echoed across the field.

Carlos ran up to Jon yelling, "You did it! You scored the winning goal. You're a winner! You can do anything if you think you can."

Jon learned many valuable lessons from Carlos. His confidence grew by tackling the tough times with effort and hard work.

Lesson Three

Tough Times

Dear _____,
When I am at home, please help me with:

_____

_____

_____

_____.

Thank you for getting me to school everyday.

Love,

_____

Lesson Three

Tough Times

Things that are difficult for me at school:

_____

_____

_____

_____

_____

What I can do when things are difficult:

_____

_____

_____

_____

_____

Lesson 4

GOALS TO IMPROVE ATTENDANCE

Lesson 4

GOALS TO IMPROVE ATTENDANCE

Lesson Four

Goals to Improve Attendance

Description:
- This lesson will teach students to set attendance goals.

Objective(s):
- Students will set goals to improve school attendance.
- Students will understand the effort needed to achieve their goals.

Estimated Time:
- 30-60 minutes

Material(s) Needed:
- Goal Sheet (see page 47)
- Home School Pledge (see page 48)
- Goal Gram Update (see page 49)
- Use poster template as a coloring page, a story starter, a what if situation or any other way that would enhance the message of the lesson.

Procedures:
- Talk about effort. What effort will it take to continue/improve my school attendance?

Lesson Four

Goals to Improve Attendance *(cont.)*

➤Discuss which of these efforts do I already make? Which do I need to improve?

➤Set specific goals and state the effort needed to achieve the goals on the Goal Sheet.

➤Complete the Home/School Pledge.

➤Complete the Parent Info gram.

Follow-up Activity:
➤Goal Gram
➤Review daily effort on worksheet
➤Review the goals that your students have set at a class meeting.
➤Celebrate with students as goals are achieved and new goals are established to improve attendance.

Personal Testimonial:
➤Share a goal you have for yourself professionally and the effort you have to put in to achieve the goal. Give an example of how you evaluate the goal.

Goals to Improve Attendance

My attendance goals

Parent will help me

I will

Parent will

Parent Info-Gram

Home/School Pledge
To meet attendance goals

Dear _____,

I will need your help in meeting my attendance goals. Together we will work hard. Together we will be successful. We CAN do it. We pledge to meet the following goals and plan.

_____
student signature

_____
parent signature

Goal Info-Gram
Update

Dear _____,
We had fun working on our goals this week.
I have really improved on _____

_____
_____. I still
need to work on_____

_____
_____. I pledge to do the
following this coming week to work on my
goals: _____

_____.

_____
student signature

Lesson 5

COMING TO SCHOOL

Lesson 5

COMING TO SCHOOL

Lesson Five

Coming to School

Description:
-In this lesson, students will learn how their absences affect others. They will learn a rap song to perform for others.

Objective(s):
-Students will understand how their absence from school affects other people.
-Students will share with classmates the attendance rap song.

Material(s) Needed:
-Flow chart (see pages 54-55)
-Rap Song Sheet (see page 56)
-Parent Info-Gram (see page 57)
-Use poster template as a coloring page, a story starter, a what if situation or any other way that would enhance the message of the lesson.

Procedures:
-Discuss how an absence affects you and other people (see flow chart page 54/55). Copy flow chart and make into overhead. Complete as you discuss.
-Have students complete a copy of the flow chart to attach to the Info-Gram to take home to parent(s).
-Share with students that you have a song and need performers (Can be done individually, in small or large group).

Lesson Five

Coming to School

➜Model the rap (see page __).
➜Assign student parts (5 students per group).
➜Practice rap.
➜Perform for others in your school or invite parents to see the performance. (Parent Info gram, see page __)

Extensions:
➜Record the song for morning school announcements.

Follow-up Discussion:
➜In partner share: have your students tell their partner how it feels when a friend is not at school (sad, worried, etc.).
➜Share responses with the whole class.

Personal Testimonial:
➜Share how student absences affects you. Emphasize the impact of their absence on your concern for their well being.

Lesson Five

Coming to School

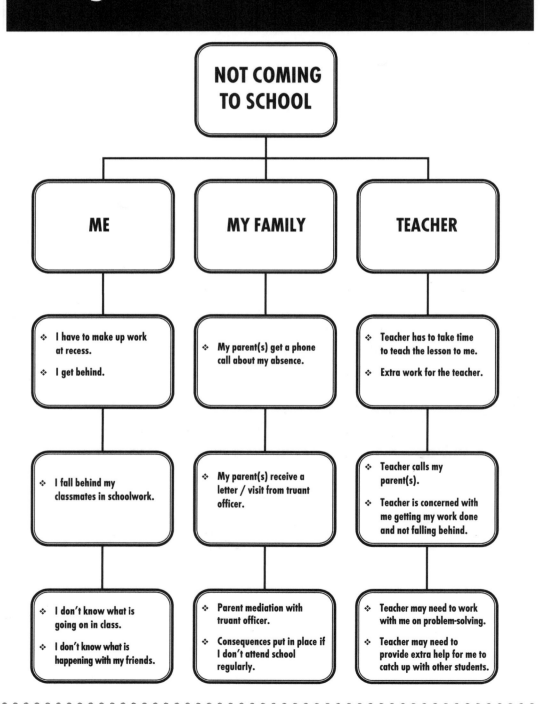

NOT COMING TO SCHOOL

ME

- ❖ I have to make up work at recess.
- ❖ I get behind.

- ❖ I fall behind my classmates in schoolwork.

- ❖ I don't know what is going on in class.
- ❖ I don't know what is happening with my friends.

MY FAMILY

- ❖ My parent(s) get a phone call about my absence.

- ❖ My parent(s) receive a letter / visit from truant officer.

- ❖ Parent mediation with truant officer.
- ❖ Consequences put in place if I don't attend school regularly.

TEACHER

- ❖ Teacher has to take time to teach the lesson to me.
- ❖ Extra work for the teacher.

- ❖ Teacher calls my parent(s).
- ❖ Teacher is concerned with me getting my work done and not falling behind.

- ❖ Teacher may need to work with me on problem-solving.
- ❖ Teacher may need to provide extra help for me to catch up with other students.

Lesson Five

Coming to School

```
            ┌─────────────────┐
            │   NOT COMING    │
            │   TO SCHOOL     │
            └─────────────────┘
                     │
     ┌───────────────┼───────────────┐
┌─────────┐    ┌─────────┐    ┌─────────┐
│         │    │         │    │         │
└─────────┘    └─────────┘    └─────────┘
     │              │              │
┌─────────┐    ┌─────────┐    ┌─────────┐
│         │    │         │    │         │
└─────────┘    └─────────┘    └─────────┘
     │              │              │
┌─────────┐    ┌─────────┐    ┌─────────┐
│         │    │         │    │         │
└─────────┘    └─────────┘    └─────────┘
     │              │              │
┌─────────┐    ┌─────────┐    ┌─────────┐
│         │    │         │    │         │
└─────────┘    └─────────┘    └─────────┘
```

 **Coming to School Rap**

Student A: Coming to School IS Really Cool

Everyone: See you everyday

Student B: I like friends and playing at school

Everyone: See you everyday

Student C: It makes me happy to be at school

Everyone: See you everyday

Student D: I like to read and learn new things

Everyone: See you everyday

Student E: I can be anything I want to be

Everyone: See you everyday…
And be real COOL!

Rap with beat.

Student Actions: Arm extended with index finger pointing to classmates with each beat.

Everyone Actions: See you everyday.

Performance –
Coming Your Way Soon!

Dear _____,

Help me memorize my part of the Coming

to School Rap. I have a big performance

on _____ at _____
       (date)   (time)

for _____.
                        (place)

Hope you want to come watch. Please let

my teacher know.

Love,

_____

Performance –
Coming Your Way Soon!

Dear _____,
(Teacher)
I would love to see the Coming to School

Rap. See you on _____

at _____.

_____
(Parent Signature)

Lesson 6

TIME MANAGEMENT

Lesson 6

TIME MANAGEMENT

Lesson Six

Time Management

Description:
-This lesson will teach students the importance of using time wisely. They will feel better about themselves and this will help their attendance to improve.

Objective(s):
-Students will brainstorm ideas for using time wisely.
-Students will understand the cause and effect of using time wisely.

Estimated Time:
30 minutes

Material(s) Needed:
-Goal sheet (see page 65)
-Parent Info-gram (see page 64)
-Use poster template as a coloring page, a story starter, a what if situation or any other way that would enhance the message of the lesson.

Procedures:
-Discuss:
   What tasks does each student need to do between the time he/she arrives at school and the beginning of class? (Hang up coat, sharpen pencils, lunch count...) Write this on large sheet of paper.

Lesson Six

Time Management *(cont.)*

How long does that take? (You can time a student doing them)
We call these tasks we do everyday routines. How can each of
you and therefore the whole class manage that time better?

➡Repeat this procedure for morning routine until recess, recess until
lunch, and after lunch, and the end of the school day routines.

➡What happens when you don't use time wisely during before
class routine?
   Morning routine?
   Before lunch routine?
   After lunch routine?
   End of Day routine?

➡What happens when you use time wisely?

➡Have students look at each sheet and journal about which part of
the day they need to use their time more wisely.

➡Have students write specific goal to work on for the next week
on the goal sheet. Make sure the goal is specific and states the
effort that will be put in and how the goal can be measured.

➡If I use my time well; I establish a routine, which helps me use
my time wisely.

Lesson Six

 **Time Management** *(cont.)*

Follow-up Activity:
➙Create a class goal for time management and revisit each day.
➙Evaluate and discuss how well your class is doing with their goal.

Personal Testimonial:
➙Share an example of how you use time wisely and the benefits you get from doing so.

Info-Gram

Time Management

Dear _____,
I would like to share with you what I
learned about routines and why they are
important. I learned: _____

_____

_____

_____

When I have a routine, I am using my time
wisely. Please help me keep my routine at
home. My teacher, _____,
will help me keep my routines at school.
Thanks! You're the greatest!

Love,

_____

Time Management

Lesson 7

Lesson 7

STUDENT RESPONSIBILITIES AT HOME

Lesson Seven

Student Responsibilities at Home

Description:
➤This lesson will teach students to recognize what their responsibilities as a student are at home. They will recognize how routines at school is related to routines at home.

Objective(s):
➤Students will create home routines for before and after school and bedtime.
➤Students will understand if they establish routine, it helps them use their time wisely.
➤Students will see the correlation between using time wisely at school and how this can be applied to home (For example: they will have more time to play.)

Estimated Time:
30 minutes

Material(s) Needed:
➤Home Routine Worksheet (see pages 73)
➤Parent Info-gram (see page 72)
➤Use poster template as a coloring page, a story starter, a what if situation or any other way that would enhance the message of the lesson.

Lesson Seven

Student Responsibilities at Home *(cont.)*

Procedures:

-Hand out Home Routine Worksheet to students. Have them complete it. (For K-2, brainstorm these ideas on the board and then have students copy them onto the worksheet.)

-Discuss and write routines on board/overhead.

-Ask students how they can improve on their routines so they are using time as wisely as possible. For example:

- •**Morning Routine**
- •Shower/bathe the night before
- •Set the alarm so you have plenty of time to eat and
  get ready for school
- •Get plenty of sleep so it is easier to get up
- •Eat a good breakfast

- •**After School Routine**
- •Eat snack
- •Do homework right away so the rest of the night is free
- •Put homework immediately back in backpack so it doesn't
  get left or misplaced
- •Put backpack by door you will leave through in the morning

- •**Bedtime Routine**
- •Shower/bathe
- •Lay clothes out
- •Set alarm
- •Put coat, shoes/boots by door

-Have students write the changes that will improve their routines in the middle box.

Lesson Seven

Student Responsibilities at Home (cont.)

Discuss:

➡ What happens when you "waste time" in the morning? (Mom/Dad upset, run late, miss breakfast, late for school, feel rushed…)

➡ What happens when you "waste time" after school? (Homework might not get done, may not get chores done)

➡ What happens when you "waste time" at bedtime? (Mom/Dad upset, tired the next day, hard to get up, might miss the bus/ride, irritable…)

➡ What happens when you use time wisely? (On time, Mom/Dad happy, calm, get everything done, ready for school…)

➡ Why is it important to use time wisely?

➡ What do you need your parents to help you with that you can't do yourself? (drive to school if don't take bus, take to childcare in the morning). Have students write who is responsible for the routine in the third column on chart.

➡ Whose responsibility is it to get ready for school on time?
   • To do homework?
   • To do chores?
   • To make sure you get enough sleep?

Lesson Seven

Student Responsibilities at Home (cont.)

Follow-up Activities:

➡Have students draw a picture of one thing they can do independently as part of their home routine. Ask them to share with the whole class.

➡Have students create home routine checklists to hang on their bedroom door.

Personal Testimonial:

➡Share how you created a routine and how this routine has helped you to meet all the responsibilities you have at home or at school.

Being Responsible

EXTRA! EXTRA!
Read All About It!

Dear _____,

Extra! Extra! Read All About It! Do you

know that I am responsible for: _____

_____

_____

_____

I know I can do these things myself. But I

do need help with some things. Will you

help me _____

_____

_____

It really means a lot to me when you help

me with things I can't do myself.

Love,

_____

Home Routine Worksheet

What I need to do each MORNING:

_____

_____

_____

_____

Whose responsibility is it?

_____

_____

_____

_____

Things I can do to improve my routine:

_____

_____

_____

_____

_____

_____

_____

Home Routine Worksheet

What I need to do each AFTERNOON:

_____

_____

_____

_____

_____

Whose responsibility is it?

_____

_____

_____

_____

Things I can do to improve my routine:

_____

_____

_____

_____

_____

_____

_____

_____

Home Routine Worksheet

What I need to do each NIGHT:

_____

_____

_____

_____

Whose responsibility is it?

_____

_____

_____

_____

Things I can do to improve my routine:

_____

_____

_____

_____

_____

_____

_____

Lesson 8

ATTENDANCE + EFFORT = SUCCESS

Lesson 8

ATTENDANCE + EFFORT = SUCCESS

Lesson Eight

Attendance + Effort = Success

Description:
-Students will understand the relationship between attendance at school and the effort they put forth in being successful.

Objective(s):
-Students will make the connection between attendance at school and being successful.
-Students will understand that success doesn't equal money but rather the opportunity to be or do whatever you desire.

Estimated Time:
-30 minutes

Material(s) Needed:
-Success Ladder (see page 83)
-Ladder steps (see page 82). Copy, laminate, and cut apart for use on the ladder.
-Money (new bills) in the following denominations: 1 - $100.00 bill, 1- $50 bill, 1 - $20 bill, 1 - $10 bill, 1 - $5 bill, 1 - $2 bill, and 1 - $1 bill. (see page 84/85)
-Use poster template as a coloring page, a story starter, a what if situation or any other way that would enhance the message of the lesson.
-Parent Info gram (see page 86)

Procedures:
-Ask the students what attendance means, what effort means.

Lesson Eight

Attendance + Effort = Success *(cont.)*

➡ Talk with students about moving up the ladder with attendance and effort to achieve success.
➡ Ask for a volunteer to help you.

First rung of ladder – reading skills. Ask what effort they had to put into learning to read (sounding out words, putting words together, practicing reading). Being in school and putting forth effort helped them to be successful in school. $1.00 – give to banker and write next to reading skills on overhead.

Second rung of ladder – ask students what other skills they learned (math, writing, spelling, etc.). Put up rung two – Other new skills. Did you need to put in effort to learn those new skills? Did you need to be in school? Attendance + Effort = Success Give the banker (volunteer) a $2 bill and write $2.00 next to rung 2 on the overhead.

Third rung – Ask students what skills we haven't talked about yet that they have learned (sharing, taking turns, working together, getting along, solving problems). Put up rung three – working with other people. How much do you think learning to work with others is worth? Give banker $5 and put on overhead. Ask banker how much money you have now.

Fourth rung – Ask students, now that you have learned to read, write, spell, math, science, social studies, and how to work with other people, what does that make you? (Better person, well rounded, smarter are possible answers they might give.) Yes, you are smarter now. Put up rung four. Ask what that is worth? Give banker $10 and write on overhead.

Lesson Eight

Attendance + Effort = Success *(cont.)*

Fifth rung – How do you show (teacher's name) that you have learned these skills? Put up Learning New skills, passing tests and moving on to the next grade. What do you think this is worth? Give $20 to banker and write on overhead. Ask banker how much money we have now.

Sixth rung – What do you think comes next on the ladder? We've learned new skills and passed from grade 4 to grade 5, now what? Put up Pass all grades. Do you need to be in school to pass all grades? Do you have to put in effort? If you are in school and put in the effort, you will be successful and pass all grades.

After ladder is completed, discuss the following with the class:
What happens after you graduate from high school? (College – talk about parents not going with you to college; Who will get you up in the morning for classes? What happens if you don't go to class? Will you need to put in effort to graduate from college? Even in college attendance + effort = success). Some students may not go to college, they may get training or go directly into a job.

Put up the next rung – job skill. What will your boss be looking for with attendance on the job? What if you come in late? (Dock pay, too many times, may get fired) What will your boss be looking for with effort? So on the job, attendance + effort = success.

If we were going to summarize what we learned today what would you say:
- Success = A Better Life
- Hard Work is Worth It
- Write on top of overhead.
- Was the money the point of this lesson? No.
- What was the point?

Lesson Eight

Attendance + Effort = Success *(cont.)*

Follow- up Discussion:

➡Ask students about to think about and then share times in their lives when they felt successful. What effort did they put forth to be successful?

Personal Testimonial:

➡Share how your efforts impact your accomplishments.

Attendance + Effort = Success

Learning new skills for job/work	$100.00

Passing all grades	$50.00

Learning new skills/Passing tests to go to next grade	$20.00

Getting smarter	$10.00

Learning to work with people	$5.00

Learning new skills	$2.00

Learning to read	$1.00

Attendance + Effort = Success

Attendance + Effort = Success

$100   ONE HUNDRED   DOLLARS $100
$100 $100

$50   FIFTY   DOLLARS $50
$50 $50

$20   TWENTY   DOLLARS $20
$20 $20

$10   TEN   DOLLARS $10
$10 $10

Attendance + Effort = Success

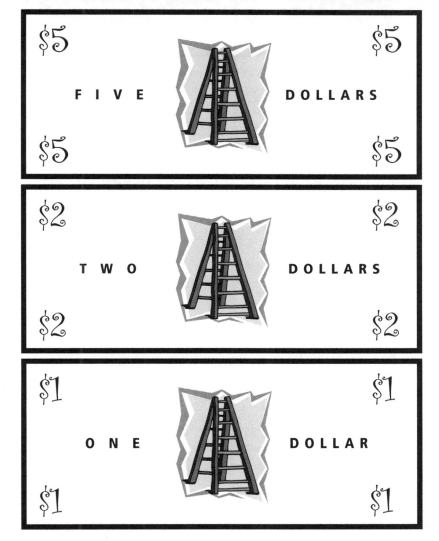

Info-Gram

Attendance + Effort = Success

Dear _____,

Did you know that attendance + effort = Success? To me, attendance + effort = success means _____

_____

_____

_____

If I were going to give this lesson a title, it would be: _____

_____

_____.

Thanks for all you do to help me be successful.

Love,

_____

Lesson 9

Lesson 9

Lesson Nine

Forward to the Future Connection

Description:
➤This lesson will teach students the connection between attendance at school and their future plans.

Objective(s):
➤Students will understand the impact of regular school attendance with their future plans.
➤Students will understand the cost of living (in their state), compare that with the potential income from future jobs they have researched and make connections about the relationship between the cost of living and wage/salary.

Estimated Time:
60 minutes

Material(s) Needed:
➤Computers
➤Career Interest Worksheet (see page 92)
➤Cost of Living Worksheet (see page 93)
➤Parent Info gram – What I Learned Note (see page 94)
➤Use poster template as a coloring page, a story starter, a what if situation or any other way that would enhance the message of the lesson.

Lesson Nine

Forward to the Future
Connection *(cont.)*

Procedures:

- Have students write down careers of interest to them.

- Have students brainstorm the components of cost of living.

- Take students to computer lab (or wherever each student will have a computer) and have them go to this website: www.acinet.org (Select Job Search Tips). Have students complete the Career Interest Worksheet.

- Then have students go to http://costofliving.com to find the costs for their state. Complete the Cost of Living Worksheet.

- Have students sign off the computers and calculate the difference in the possible salary of one career interest and the total cost of living for one year. Discuss what they found.

- What do students notice about the years of education required and the salary they make?

- How does this relate to coming to school?

Lesson Nine

Forward to the Future Connection

Modifications:

➡For younger grades, teach the students what things are part of the cost of living (electricity, water, housing, food/grocery, phone, transportation (car + insurance + gas), Internet, TV (cable, dish, etc.), laundry, health, etc.) and how we pay for these things.

Personal Testimonial:

➡Share your why you choose your profession and how it impacts your life.

Follow-up activity:

➡Have students list things they will have to do to reach their career goals and share with each other.
➡Have students write questions for a guest speaker to come and discuss their career choice with the students.

Career Interests Worksheet

Career: _____ Salary: _____

Education requirements: _____

_____

Type of classes needed: _____

_____

Career: _____ Salary: _____

Education requirements: _____

_____

Type of classes needed: _____

_____

Career: _____ Salary: _____

Education requirements: _____

_____

Type of classes needed: _____

_____

Cost of Living Worksheet

Housing _____

Electricity _____

Heat _____

Water _____

Phone/Cell _____

Transportation _____

Car Insurance _____

Gas _____

Food/Grocery _____

TV _____

Internet _____

Clothes _____

Health _____

Laundry _____

Total _____

X 12 = _____

YEARLY
TOTAL $ _____

Info-Gram

Forward to the Future Connection

Dear _____,

Today we studied about careers and the cost of living. I'm interested in being:

_____

I learned the things that are part of what it costs to live. These things include _____

_____

_____. The average

cost of living in _____ is

_____ for one year. Thanks for

all you do to provide me with _____

_____.

Love,

_____

Lesson 10

INTERVIEW

Lesson Ten

Interview

Description:
-Students will understand how their parents view the importance of school.

Objective(s):
-Students will learn why coming to school is important to their parents.

Estimated Time:
-30 minutes

Material(s) Needed:
-Interview Sheet (see page 99/100)
-Use poster template as a coloring page, a story starter, a what if situation or any other way that would enhance the message of the lesson.

Lesson Ten

Interview

Procedures:
- Assign students to interview a parent/guardian and complete the interview handout.
- Discuss the results of each interview question.
- What did you learn about why your parents see coming to school as important?
- How does this compare with why you think school is important? (from Lesson 2)

Follow-up activity:
- Create a poster on Why Coming to School Is Important!
- Create a poster on What You Have Learned about Good School Attendance.
- Share your student's interviews with another class in your building.

Personal Testimonial:
- Share how coming to work is important to you and why it's important to be on time.

Interview

I'm Ace Reporter, _____

and I'm here to interview you about school.

What was your favorite thing about school?

_____

_____

_____

Did you have a favorite teacher? _____

What was his/her name? _____

What did you like about him/her?

_____

_____

Interview *(cont.)*

Do you remember the names of your friends?

_____

_____

What did you and your friends do for fun?

_____

_____

_____

_____

Why do you think it's important to go to school?

_____

_____

_____

Thank you for taking the time to talk with me today.

References

Baker, D. & Jansen J. (2000). Keeping kid in school: *The impact of the truancy provisions in Washington's 1995 Becca Bill*. Olympia, WA: Washington State Institute for Public Policy.

Baker, M. L., Sigmon, J. N., & Nugent, M. E. (2001). *Truancy reduction: Keeping students in school*. Washington, D.C.: U.S. Department of Justice, Office of Juvenile Justice and Delinquency Prevention.

Blum, R., Beuhring and Rinehart, (2000).

Bryk, A. S. & Thurm, Y.M. (1989). The effects of high school organization on dropping out: An exploratory investigation. *American Educational Research Journal*, 26 (3), 353-383.

Ford, J. & Sutphen, R.D. (1996). Early intervention to improve atendance in elementary school for at-risk children: A pilot program. *Social Work in Education*, 19(2), 95-102.

Henderson, A.T. & Mapp, K.L. (2002). *A new wave of evidence: The impact of school, family and community connection on students achievement* (Annual syntheses), Austin, TX: Southwest Educational Development Laboratory, National Center for Family & Community Connections with Schools.

Holbert, T., Wu, L., & Stark, M. (2002). *School attendance initiative. The first 3 years: 1998/99-2000/01.*Salem, OR: Oregon Department of Human Services, &Portland, OR: Multnomah Country, Office of School & Community Partnerships.

Huizinga, D., Loeber, R., & Thornberry, T.P. (1997). *Urban Delinquency and Substance Abuse: Initial Findings*, OJJDP, December 1997.

Huizinga, D., Loeber, R., Thornberry, T.P. and Cothern,L. (2000). "Co-occurrence of Delinquency and Other Problem Behaviors," *Juvenile Justice Bulletin*, OJJDP, November, 2000.

Lan, W. & Lanthier, R. (2003). Changes in students' academic performance and perceptions of school and self before dropping out of schools. *Journal of Education for Students Placed at Risk, 8(3), 309-332.*

Lee, V.E. & Burkam, D.T. (2003). Dropping out of high school: The role of school organization and structure. *American Educational Research Journal, 40(2), 353-393.*

References

Loeber R. & Farrington, D.P. (2000). "Young Children Who Commit Crime: Edpidemiology, Developmental Origins, Risk Factors, Early Interventions, and Policy Implications," *Development and Psychopathology, v. 12, pp. 737-762.*

National Center for Educational Statistics, (2002). Indicator 17: Students' absence from school. In *The condition of education, 2002 (pp. 40-41, 71, 159-160, 274.)* Washington DC: U.S. Department of Education.

Vernez, Georges, Krop, Richard A., Rydell, C. Peter. (1999). *Closing the Education Gap: Benefits and Costs,* Rand Mr-1036-EDU, 1999.

U.S. Department of Health and Human Services, (2001). *Youth Violence: A Report of the Surgeon General,* Rockville, MD: U.S. Department of Health and Human Services, Centers for Disease Control and Prevention, National Center for Injury Prevention and Control; Substance Abuse and Mental Health Services Administration, Center for Mental Health Services; and National Institutes of Health, National Institute of Mental Health.

About the Authors:

Sandy Ragona, MSEd, is an elementary school counselor at J.F. Kennedy School in Dubuque, Iowa with 27 years experience in school counseling. Sandy has been an adjunct professor at Loras College, Drake University, and Morningside College all in Iowa. She has led numerous workshops and training sessions locally and nationally. She is the author of the book "Eliminating Bullying" and "Please Stop I Don't Like That"

Stef Weber, MA, has taught, counseled and coached students K-12 for the past thirty years. She has been a counselor for 28 years, eight at the high school level and twenty at the elementary level. Stef has been an adjunct professor of psychology and education at Northeast Iowa Community College and Clarke College in Dubuque, Iowa.